YOU

Deserve

IT

A Journey of Life Experiences to Affirm Your Mental and Emotional Development

MYCHAL A. WINTERS, ED.S.

YOU DESERVE IT

A Journey of Life Experiences to Affirm Your Mental and Emotional Development

Copyright ©2021 by Mychal A. Winters, Ed.S.

Dedication

This book is dedicated to the Author and Creator, who has given me life and made me in His image. May this work reflect you and your glory!

This book is dedicated to my amazing firstborn son, Gabriel. Son, when you are able to read and comprehend this, I pray that you are reminded of how much I love you and how proud I am to be your father! I want you to know that you are equipped and capable of achieving whatever you put your mind and effort into. Keep God first in all things; He is your strength!

This book is dedicated to my parents, Dr.'s Michael and Kimberly Winters. Thank you for raising me to be a man of God. Thank you for loving me and caring for me even when my choices did not reflect the values you

i

instilled in me. Thank you for giving me tough love even when I felt it was too tough at times. It has shaped me to be the man I am today and the man I am constantly evolving into. To my mother, Janie Andrews, thank you for giving me life! Thank you for always cheering me on and for always being in my corner. I hope I have made you proud!

I dedicate this book to my grandparents Herman and Mary Winters. You have been the epitome of grace! You were there to guide me during the darkest and hardest times in my life. You taught me what it is to be compassionate and to speak to the best in everyone. Most important, thank you for teaching me how to win! To my grandmother, Mae Pearl Andrews, thank you for your gentleness, kindness, and generosity. I hope that my life and work reflect those values you exemplify.

I dedicate this book to my siblings Shunn Morris, Jr. and Victoria Winters. My life has been an open book to both of you. I hope you can learn from the many chapters you have witnessed firsthand, whether up close or distant. I love you both dearly and hope you manifest the lives that you aspire to have!

Finally, this book is dedicated to my village. My village consists of extended family, classmates, associates, coworkers, students, and anyone who has interacted with me in an influential or impactful way.

YOU DESERVE IT

Thank you for our shared experiences and I hope this work makes you proud!

Contents

Introduction

This book was written during the hardest season of my life. I wanted to share that detail so that as you read this book, you will understand that it is not coming from someone with life figured out or has it all together. One of my good friends once told me that pain is a motivator. My greatest pain motivated me to write this book. Pain also creates an opportunity for healing. Hence the title, *You Deserve It*. Writing has always been one of my strengths, and I hope that sharing some of my personal experiences through my gift of writing inspires someone who has been through similar experiences. I also hope I inspire someone to pursue their dreams in the face of adversity. This book was inspired by the trails of life and the valuable lessons learned along the way.

During the process of healing, I learned how to truly love myself because that is all I have. I learned how to separate my self-worth from other people's words and actions. Through counseling, I learned that I had a lot more going right than I did wrong. That process taught me to accept myself fully and to celebrate myself. I witnessed the faithfulness of God. Sometimes, I struggled financially, and He always made a way for me to have what I needed either through extra work, opportunities to earn extra money, and support from my parents and grandparents. That process taught me not to have expectations of others and to live free from other's decisions. During my healing journey, I realized that I deserved to live life and to live it abundantly. I deserved to be healthy and to have a healthy love life. I learned to embrace my failures and to love again.

During the time I wrote this book, I also had COVID-19, along with having asthma. I was temporarily unemployed, despite being highly qualified in my field of work. On top of all of that, I earned a Specialist in Education (Ed.S.) and began my first semester as a doctoral student. My life is full of wins and lessons. The content and ideals shared in this book are meant to be a guide. I do not share these things to gain "clout" or to make anyone feel sorry for me. If I can survive the darkest moments of my life and still smile, pursue my goals, and encourage others, you can do anything you put your mind to! And you deserve to do it!

This book is also a book of healing. I have immersed myself in a healing process over the past two years. I learned that I deserve everything that I had and everything that I desired. My current state of being reflects the energy that I put out and the energy I nurture. You deserve all that you desire and all that you have. Thank you for your support and for spending time with me by reading this book. I hope it is helpful to you in some way. Enjoy.

CHAPTER I

Resilient

I n this life, we are never guaranteed success. We are never guaranteed that our dreams and desires will become our reality. We will, however, experience hard times, disappointment, pain, and loss. I have a theory that if you can be resilient between difficult seasons, you can conquer each situation as it comes and remain mentally and emotionally strong. Some situations test your strength more than others, but the key is to keep going. I am a firm believer that whatever has been lost can be replaced with much better. Whatever you have failed miserably at can provide you with the pathway for success. I am a firm believer that whatever painful experiences you have endured can guide your healing and can help others. The way to turn unfortunate experiences is to be resilient. Being resilient begins in the mind. To recover from or adjust to change or misfortune, you must have a mindset open to adapt to change.

Life is constantly changing. It is easy to become stagnant while the world is constantly evolving. I can recall seasons of my life where I became stagnant because I allowed fear and pain to paralyze me. I had to change my perspective and response to fear and pain to overcome the situations I had found myself in. I allowed negative thoughts and feelings to live in my mind rent-free and they controlled how I interacted with the world around me. Those negative thoughts and feelings resulted from me not addressing areas in which I had failed and I got stuck there. My thoughts and feelings shifted when I learned that situations do not define me. I embraced the truth that my response to life's challenges determines my outcome. I also had to learn that it is quite normal to make many mistakes. It is a part of living. Often, I made situations more critical than they actually were. With this resilient mindset, I perceived each situation as a learning opportunity instead of a defining moment.

YOU DESERVE IT

You deserve to be resilient and adapt to change. Change is inevitable. Resilience over time can lead to growth. You deserve to shift your mindset to see the opportunities to win and grow in each situation.

CHAPTER II

Health

As a child, I suffered from having severe asthma attacks and being hospitalized several times due to asthma and pneumonia. As an adult, I have had episodes where I had to be taken to the ER, but those occasions were rare and I can manage it. In 2020, there was an outbreak of coronavirus, also known as COVID-19. I am also a COVID-19 survivor. That year has taught me the importance of maintaining good health. Mental and emotional health is equally important and physical health. I strongly believe that they are not mutually exclusive. I believe that we all have had our share of dramatic experiences in 2020. We all have experienced loss and gain, and significant life changes personally and economically. These experiences have affected our health, whether emotional, mental, or physical.

2020 was all over the place for me. I experienced two career changes, being temporarily unemployed, business failure, starting a new business, divorce, completing the first semester of doctoral courses, a new relationship, traveling, going broke, receiving lump sums of money, becoming infected with COVID-19, losing over 60 pounds, and the list goes on. These experiences have taken a toll on my health in some way. Most people would not have survived a fraction of these traumatic, life-impacting situations. I am reminded of a saying used by my high-school football coaches, "tough times don't last, tough people do."

Having COVID-19 put some things in perspective for me. It taught me how fragile life truly is and that I am not untouchable. With that realization, I prioritized my health; physical, mental, and emotional. I realized that if I died, some things would continue and others would not be the same. The areas of my life that would continue with little or no impact if I were unhealthy or not alive, I prioritize less. The areas that would be highly affected are highly prioritized. I am thankful to have experienced that because it has heightened my awareness of what is truly important.

What if you don't have the strength or the health to be tough? It is perfectly fine if you do not. You deserve to be healthy emotionally, mentally, and physically. You deserve to be honest with yourself and your current state. It is ok and very healthy to admit that your health is not what it once was or what you would like for it to be. It is ok to be angry, sad, upset, confused, happy, excited, or whatever you feel. You deserve to feel what you feel. It is ok to process your thoughts. Those things do not define you, but how you respond to them does define you. Your response and attitude to life's challenges leave an imprint in the universe. You deserve to leave a healthy legacy and imprint in this lifetime and those to come.

CHAPTER III

Education

E ducation has always been a priority for me. I can recall as a young child, before starting formal school, my father would have me practice writing my name and other family members going over words and reading with me. My grandfather used to reward me for good grades by taking me out to my favorite place. Even now, he still acknowledges my academic achievements. My parents were always strict with me about school. Their expectation was always high achievement because they knew that I could achieve at a high level. As an educator, I emphasize the importance of education daily. Some associate education with simply going to school and getting good grades. I associate getting an "education" with gaining knowledge through life-changing experiences. Learning only takes place when changes occur. Once you gain knowledge, you are responsible for it and you must act on it. Enlightenment breeds action. This is the type of education I value and hope that my students and those around me will value. Just because you attend school, get good grades, and a degree does not mean you truly have an education.

I associate education with growth. We are all constantly growing and evolving as life experiences shift. Personal growth and development will require a different view and approach to accessing certain information. Growth also requires a different response to information. When this happens, we can observe growth in our thinking. One of my educational monikers is "The Growth Educator." I use that name to reflect my disposition about personal growth. The name is not about quantitative growth in terms of assessment data (although I do have the data to support evidence of that type of growth), but it is about how I seek to help those I encounter to grow in their mindset. I aim to help others develop a growth mindset and to see the possibilities in each situation.

I could write a book about the lack of motivation that young black and brown boys have towards school. But to be honest, I do not blame them. In fact, I am them. They have that attitude because they aren't actually learning anything that they deem useful. It is easy to tell a scholar that they need to learn about the main idea of a text, slope-intercept form, and that the mitochondria are the powerhouse of the cell, but then what? How does that information make them feel better about themselves? How does it add value to them? How will it immediately affect them? There are not enough anchor charts in the world to change a child's state of being. As an educator, I seek to teach young minds how to access any type of information and how to process it. Some information may seem less useful than others, but I strive to relay the message they need to process it and know how to categorize the information regardless of how they feel about it. I would be remised if I failed to teach those young minds how to craft information and turn it into knowledge. Most minority students are not aware of the odds against them. My mindset is that the process of learning will always be more consistent than the content. If I can educate them about the process, they can master any type of content.

Teaching virtually has certainly been a challenge, but it has helped me become more solution-oriented. Trying to keep middle-schoolers engaged and motivated daily is a task in itself, but to do it virtually takes a special skill. Regardless of how tired, frustrated, or indifferent I may feel, I owe it to each scholar to give them my best daily.

Unfortunately, I see a trend where scholars are valuing education less and less. It almost seems as if we have to perform tricks to get them to even pay attention. There are so many non-essential things that take their attention away from learning, and unfortunately, those distractions are encouraged by some of the parents. The hard reality is that the system is designed to keep our minority scholars distracted. The less educated our scholars are, the harder it will be for them to truly succeed in life. My ultimate goal is to educate the minds of our youth and get them to grow academically and personally. The lightbulb may not come on with me, but I at least want to show them where the light switch is.

The most valuable lessons I have learned in life have resulted in changed behaviors and attitudes. If I have ever walked away from a relationship, friendship, activity, organization, etc., it is because I learned more valuable information about myself that revealed that the connection no longer served me (or never did), or that I did not have a purpose that served it well enough (in my own estimate). Anything that I have ever pursued resulted from some form of information or an ideal I believed to be true and needed to be acted upon. Yes, school is important, getting good grades is important, getting the degree is important, but what truly moves you? What calls you to action? Those are the areas that will educate you the most. They will teach you about yourself and the world around you. You deserve to be educated and to educate those around you.

CHAPTER IV

Faith

Growing up, church was always a big deal to my family. I grew up seeing them active in the church and living out their beliefs as well. My family has always emphasized belief in God. That is something that I have learned to value personally. I did go through a period of time where I did not value that relationship because of personal issues I had with other individuals who were influential when it came to my beliefs. As I matured, I learned to separate my personal beliefs from my personal relationships with others.

Some people have the misconception that religion and faith are the same. Two people can have the same religion but exercise different faith. Because we are all different, our beliefs and perspectives will be different. How we process and respond to information will be different. Because of the differences in how we perceive information, there can be discrepancies in how the truth is perceived. A common trend now is for people to have their "own truth." That viewpoint makes the truth subjective. As it relates to religious beliefs, people should follow their own convictions.

Regardless of an individual's religious background, who and what they believe in and how they believe is a right that should be respected. We all have some type of faith in something. You deserve to have something and someone to believe in. Depending on what source you use to define the word, faith can have many meanings. The definition that helps me conceptualize faith the most is the substance of things hoped for and the evidence of things not seen. As an educator, I like to use key words to help develop understanding. From that definition, the words substance, hope, and evidence stand out.

You deserve to receive the evidence of the substance you are hoping for. The belief you will receive evidence of the substance you hope for is your faith. There will always be an area in your life you desire to find evidence of a certain substance, whether it be health, financial, relational, personal, professional, academic, etc. Always remain hopeful and never stop believing! Sometimes the evidence (your reality) may not match the substance you are hoping for. Faith is the belief they will align. Have faith and take the necessary actions until it aligns! Faith and hard work will manifest it. You deserve it!

CHAPTER V

Hustle

G rowing up, my passion was to be the best football player I could be. I always knew there was someone else better than me on the team and/or at my position, but I always strived to work as hard as I could. My willingness to be adaptable and work hard to meet the needs of the team allowed me to gain experience playing multiple positions. Over the years, that determination and hustle helped me to stand out as a hard worker. I learned to apply that determination and hustle mentality to other areas of my life.

A person that knows how to hustle knows how to win. I mastered the art of winning by creating my own set of goals and achieving those goals. Once I created those goals, I followed the steps to achieve them step by step, day by day. I did not allow setbacks, fear, or doubt keep me from achieving those goals. I always knew exactly what I wanted to do and how to execute it.

One thing I did not care for but was part of the game was comparison. I would always be compared to another player at the same position. I feared that my gifts and talents would not measure up against the next person. That drove me to work even harder. I did small things to make myself stand out from the others. I still deal with comparison today. I learned a long time ago there are others around me working just as hard, if not harder, at the same thing I want to accomplish. I can't compare myself to the next. My journey, my process, and the small things that only I can do are what separates me from the rest. I trust the process and know that I will get what I hustle for.

You deserve to hustle hard until you achieve your goals. Be working toward achieving your own goals you have set, and not a set of goals that someone else has given you. You deserve to put all of the energy and intensity you put toward someone else's job or team into your own goals and dreams. Sometimes you may have to modify your goals and that's ok! There will be some people who are supposed to help guide you but actually tear you down. Stay focused. Don't expect those who are on the same or similar path as you to clap for you or to genuinely support you. Just like in sports, some people see you as the competition and opposition. Be a good sport and cheer them on and encourage them anyway. Don't be afraid to learn a new skill. The more you work at something new, the better you will become at it. But your hustle will determine your success and will make people respect your craft. You deserve to work smart and hustle hard!

CHAPTER VI

Purpose

One of the most frequently asked questions is, what is my purpose? There are endless amounts of books, YouTube videos, podcasts, curriculums, trainings, etc., on purpose. For some reason, there is a misconception that purpose is a specific task you were put on earth to do and if you do not have that one specific thing identified by a certain point, you will have failed at life. I am so thankful that that is not true!

I am not a "purpose" guru, but I firmly believe that who you are, where you are, and what you are doing is part of your "purpose." The people you are around every day and how you interact with them is your purpose. Your purpose is carried out daily. In that estimation, we each have our own individual purpose we fulfill each day. It is not something to be discovered; it is to be unpacked. All of your desires and dispositions are indicators of your purpose. What you do with them will determine where your "purpose" will lead you. Therefore it is so important to be in tune with yourself. Do not allow another soul in this universe to convince you or tell you what your purpose is because they did not give it to you! We will spend the rest of our lives unpacking our purpose. Each season of life will unlock a new layer of purpose as we engage in new experiences that will require new approaches in how we interact with life. The more that we learn about ourselves, the more knowledgeable we will become about how to be purposeful in the world each day. Again, that will change as often as the seasons change, but the core aspects will remain the same. Stay true to who you are at the core.

The world is a big place, but we are all connected in many ways. You may think that you were put here to do a specific task, but you may overlook the impact you have on the lives of those around you by doing the simplest task. You never know who is watching and what they are watching.

YOU DESERVE IT

You have a purpose and you deserve to live it out each day. You deserve to share your purpose with the world and those around you. You deserve to learn more about yourself and your purpose each day.

CHAPTER VII

Never Settle

Have you ever purchased a meal and it came out wrong, missing part of the order, or was cold? I'm sure you took it back, as you should have. How many times do we accept the incorrect order or the cold food because it would be more convenient than the hassle of taking it back? How often do we settle because it is more convenient to accept what is undesirable than to wait for what we truly want? This can apply to relationships, careers, friendships, personal goals, etc.

When we settle, we accept less than what we deserve due to convenience. From my own experiences, I always knew when I was settling in relationships, jobs, friendships, and personal goals. I was fully aware when I was accepting conditions that were not suitable for me, but because it was convenient, I made them good enough.

Choosing not to settle simply means to not accept less than you have given. It is easy to settle for less because it is convenient. But does it truly serve you well? Will it be an inconvenience to you in the long run? I learned that not all relationships can reciprocate, and no one is at fault for that. Not all relationships can grow and be healthy, and that is ok. It's not okay to settle for those types of relationships when you know you desire more. It's not okay to settle for those relationships because you're lonely and "everybody needs somebody." Settling for dead-end relationships where reciprocation, kindness, respect, and commitment are missing will cost you in the long run.

Just as important it is to never settle for less, you also shouldn't settle on giving your best in relationships, friendships, career, and personal goals. When you become familiar with a person or activity, you can get into a routine. Sometimes you can get so caught up in the routine that you become less sensitive to the needs of those around you.

Stay alert and always strive to give your best to those around you because they deserve the best from you! Just like you don't want to settle, don't make those who depend on you settle either. You deserve to have meaningful relationships and friendships, and you deserve to bring good energy to those around you. You deserve the best and to give your best!

CHAPTER XIII

Commitment

As a young boy, I can remember my father telling me, "Son, sometimes things will get worse before they get better." As an adult, I have learned that the bridge between worse and better is commitment. Any time that I have failed greatly at something, it is because I was not committed to attaining the desired results. Discipline is a component of commitment. Wherever you lack discipline is an indicator of where you lack commitment. Commitment is what keeps you on the job when you are no longer passionate about the work. It is what keeps you focused when you do not get any recognition.

35

Commitment is what keeps you going hard at practice even when you don't get the playing time you want. Commitment is what keeps you and your spouse together when the feeling of love is gone. Commitment is the glue that holds your life together when you feel like giving up. Again, there is no commitment without discipline.

Commitment transcends feelings. Life is not always about doing what feels good. Making critical decisions based on feelings is highly unstable and irresponsible. Your feelings will change as often as you change underwear. Commitment is a hard decision you must make daily regardless of how you feel. Commitment is saying no matter how I feel or how hard it gets, I believe in myself, what I am doing can succeed and I will not give up until this situation manifests into what I want it to be.

If you are in a relationship or marriage, you will not always have the feeling of "being in love" with your partner. You deserve to be honest with yourself and with your partner so you can address the issues together and move forward in a loving and productive way.

You deserve commitment and to be committed. If you are pursuing a goal or dream, you deserve to be committed to the process. If you are in a relationship or marriage, you deserve to have a partner committed to you and working on improving the situation regardless of how you "feel." You deserve to put your feelings aside and be disciplined in achieving what your heart and mind desire.

CHAPTER IX

Life

One of my favorite books has a line that says, "I come to bring life, and life more abundantly." I can reflect on my life and observe the times where I did not value it. I can recall times where things did not go my way and I felt like I did not deserve to be on this earth. Fortunately, I now know better and understand that a bad day does not mean a bad life. A bad season does not mean a bad life. A bad few years does not mean a bad life. Do not be so quick to throw away everything that has so much meaning because of a temporary season of discomfort. I hope to encourage someone feeling that their life does not matter and tell them you were created for and with a purpose. You deserve the life you were given, and you deserve to live it abundantly. You deserve to realize that your "abundantly" may not look like someone else's abundantly and that is perfectly ok. Your life is not meant to be compared to anyone else's. Learn to love the season you are in and master the season you are in. Be thankful for all things and prepare to be blessed and walk in your next season of life. God has a way of slowing us down when we do not appreciate where we are and what we have. Some take it as punishment, but your response will determine whether you will pass the test. Always respond to life with gratitude and thanks. If you cannot see the abundance you have, how will you be able to appreciate that which you desire? Life is short, so make it meaningful.

CHAPTER X

Dream

I will forever appreciate my parents for encouraging me to pursue my goals and dreams. I also appreciate them for being great examples and pursuing theirs. Everyone has a dream and everyone is entitled to their dream. My question is, do you know how to accurately interpret your dreams? I have the unique gift of prophetic dreams. Since I was a child, I have had supernatural encounters and dreams filled with meaning that has helped someone I shared them with. With any gift comes great responsibility. It would be reckless for me to think that the dreams and visions I had were literal. I had to write them down, analyze them and interpret them. I had to research symbolism and meanings. I had to analyze the people in the dreams and their purposes in that role in the dream. Not everything is literal. I shared that to say, not every dream and desire you have is literal. Be responsible enough to analyze your dreams and desires. I will give you an example. Growing up, like most young black boys, I wanted to play in the NFL. I played football from fourth grade through my senior year of high school. Never played a down of college ball and did not go pro, but I still accomplished my dreams. I was infatuated with the jersey sales, signing the big contract, being seen on TV, and having my highlights shown on ESPN. So ultimately, I realized that I actually had no desire to commit myself to the process of actually putting in the necessary work to become a pro. If I wanted to, I could have committed my life to doing that and would very well have found a way, but I was responsible enough to analyze my dreams. What I truly wanted was the experience of performing well at something, contributing to a larger goal, being connected to a team, being the best in my area, having a unique skillset, being recognized for my talent and hard work, and being active and healthy. In that perspective, I could do those things in any field. I realized that I could create a life of endless success by pursuing those things I truly desired and applying those principles wherever I chose to go. That is the key to success. That is the key to living out your dreams. You deserve to find out exactly what it is you want to contribute to the world around you. You deserve to be responsible with and for your dreams. You deserve to analyze what you want out of life and to pursue it with everything that is within you.

About the Author

A uthor Mychal A. Winters, Ed.S. is an educator in Memphis, TN. Winters began his journey as an educator in 2011 as a paraprofessional in his hometown of Vicksburg, MS. It was there where he discovered his passion for working with students. He went on to earn a Bachelor of Science in Elementary Education (2015) and Master of Education in Elementary Education (2017) from Delta State University. In 2019, he earned a Specialist in Educational Administration and Leadership from The University of Southern Mississippi. In 2019, Winters founded Winters Literacy LLC, which is an educational business that provides services such as tutoring, mentoring, books and curriculum, and podcasts.

Connect

www.wintersliteracy.org

info@wintersliteracy.org

Follow

Instagram: @thegrowtheducator

Facebook: www.facebook.com/youdeserveit.info

YouTube: The Growth Educator

Wins & Lessons Podcast

Cover Photograph by Chris Cohran

Instagram: @aristoshots

Made in the USA
Middletown, DE
20 February 2021